MINISTERING
Deliverance
TO Children

With Pastor Michael Edwards

Over 100 prayer points to break the hold of the enemy over your children, and set them on the divine path of destiny!

Isa 49:25 But thus saith the Lord,... for I will contend with him that contendeth with thee, and I will save thy children. I will save thy children.

Ministering Deliverance to Children

Published by: VOICE OF COMFORT Publisher
UK: VOICE OF COMFORT, P.O. BOX 63446
SE16 3YG
UK Telephone: (+44)7412354175; (+44)(0)2036388169
©2013 Michael Edwards

Website: www.voiceofcomfort.net

E-mail : admin@voiceofcomfort.net

All scriptures, unless otherwise stated, are taken from the King James Version of the Bible.

All rights reserved.
No part of this publication may be reproduced or stored in a retrieved system or be transmitted in any form or by means mechanical, electronic, photocopying or otherwise without the prior written consent of the copyright owner.

ISBN: 978-1-908386-17-5

Isa 49:25 But thus saith the Lord,… for I will contend with him that contendeth with thee, and I will save thy children. I will save thy children.

DEDICATION

I would like to dedicate this work to my greatest mentors on earth my parents, may grace be multiplied unto you! And to the immortal invisible and only wise God.

Isa 49:25 But thus saith the Lord,… for I will contend with him that contendeth with thee, and I will save thy children. I will save thy children.

INHERITANCE
Blessing and Responsibilities
Ps 127:3

Lo, children are an heritage of the LORD: and the fruit of the womb is his reward. 4 As arrows are in the hand of a mighty man; so are children of the youth. 5 Happy is the man that hath his quiver full of them: they shall not be ashamed, but they shall speak with the enemies in the gate.

This above scripture clearly expresses the fact that just as we do not have to pay for an inheritance that comes from our parents, it is the same way children are free gifts from God. However, each inheritance comes with blessings and responsibilities. In the same manner, God expects parents to be spiritually responsible for their children. Some people say that children do not need deliverance. I could not disagree more. Parents have a solemn responsibility to provide
protection for their offspring in the matter of spiritual warfare. So many curses, legal holds,

> Isa 49:25 But thus saith the Lord,... for I will contend with him that contendeth with thee, and I will save thy children. I will save thy children.

and other legal

grounds can be inherited through the ignorance, curiosity and/or wilful disobedience of the parent. In addition to the above, our society provides a climate for demon infestation.

An inheritance is surely a pedestal to him who receives it. In other words, you begin to enjoy and live in the labour of another: an inheritance increases your wealth and strength.

In the same way children are an inheritance given by God to us, as a pedestal to lift us up, that is why the Bible states in verse 5 of the passage above that children are like arrows in the hand of a mighty man. In other words, our child is meant to project us and cross boundaries that we cannot cross and reach heights that we could not reach in our youthful days. Unfortunately for many parents, children have

become a burden and a snare, almost like a curse to them, some because their children have grown up bringing them into disrepute, others because the enemy has attacked their children with ill health and thus made them a constant burden with no peace of mind to the parents.

Others have not met the expectations of their parents and that of God for their lives; instead their many strides of success have been coloured dark with failure and multiple errors at different stages. Some children are unable to complete what they start; some drop out of school and some join bad gangs or are even initiated into cults or secret societies.

The reason for these and many more woes that befall children is not farfetched because the answer is in that passage above. Firstly, the Bible calls children an inheritance from God; like most inheritances, there will be factors that will contend and contest the right of the parents to receive this blessing.

Secondly, the Bible states they are like arrows. An arrow is an offensive weapon. The enemy knows that and will not watch you build up dangerous arsenals to devastate him eventually. This fact is very interesting because it clearly implies that the fact that children are born is proof that the adversary has vested interest in them, to make sure that they do not become effective enough to be a threat to his kingdom.

He therefore attacks children with all sorts to afflict them and cripple their destiny!
The same scripture expatiates further by saying that our children are born to speak with the enemies at the gate!

In the Bible days, the cities had gates and wise men and magistrates sat at the gates of the cities to settle disputes. Creditors also waited at the gate, to lend money and ask for money owed to them. In the former situation children were witnesses in judicial courts, also children were proof of credit worthiness.

There were also pirates outside the gates of the city seeking to attack merchants travelling in and out of the city; a man with children had strength and power to resist the enemy. The enemy knows this and will fight tooth and nail to make sure that your children cannot stand against him.

PHAROAH ON THE RAMPAGE
Catch them young (while they are upon the stool) Ex 1:16

And he said, When ye do the office of a midwife to the Hebrew women, and see them upon the stools; if it be a son, then ye shall kill him: but if it be a daughter, then she shall live.

The Bible tells us here that pharaoh commanded children to be killed at the point of delivery; here we see the enemy launching an attack against children from the infant stage (WHILE ON THE STOOL), this spirit of pharaoh is still on the rampage today.

I was driving one day and I saw little kids being led by their teacher from school on a trip somewhere. When

I asked where they were going, the teacher told me they were going to see the latest witchcraft sensation movie.

This irony is amazing because, in these same schools, prayers and expressions of love for Jesus have been banned. Our children are being taught and schooled in witchcraft but are told that mentioning the name of Jesus is offensive.

This is why we have problems with parents who do not see anything wrong with their children celebrating Halloween (a witchcraft festival) but have problems with bringing their children to church.

For some, their children have all kinds of toys and books about evil and witchcraft but not a single Bible story book.

The enemy is on a rampage to catch our children young; the battle is on whether or not you believe it. You must take hold of the weapons of war and fight the inevitable battle for both the sanctity of your home and deliverance of your children! If parents wait until the child is grown up before attempting deliverance, they will discover the enemy has wasted no time and has burrowed in deeply, often scarring body and mind. They will work tirelessly to put a child in bondage, drag him out into the world, and enslave him with many sinful habits. An

ounce of prevention here is certainly worth the proverbial 'pound of cure'.
There are many ways the enemy tries to catch children young, and demonize, possess or pervert their destiny-some of which we will examine.

NEED FOR CHILDREN'S DELIVERANCE
Gen 3:16

Unto the woman he said, I will greatly multiply thy sorrow and thy conception; in sorrow thou shalt bring forth children; and thy desire shall be to thy husband, and he shall rule over thee.

The Bible states here that there is pain in conception as well as in childbirth, because of the pains and discomfort that surround conception, many women utter words of woes while they are pregnant and all these words have a great level of influence upon the destiny of children.
This is the reason why pregnant women must learn to speak to the baby in their womb, read the bible to them, and speak prophetic words to them in the womb.

Violent words, expressions of anger and sorrow affect the lives of children in the womb.

Words also spoken at the point of delivery and naming of a child can make or mar the destiny of a child; this is one way through which evil creeps in and the devil gains a foothold and cripples the destiny of a new baby.

Jabez in the above scripture was a man who was troubled and could not succeed until God delivered him, because at the point of his birth, the pangs of delivery made his mother speak ill words and thus made his destiny ill!

A similar situation happened in the following scripture:

Gen 35:16

... And Rachel travailed, and she had hard labour.

17 And it came to pass, when she was in hard labour, that the midwife said unto her, Fear not; thou shalt have this son also.

18 And it came to pass, as her soul was in departing, (for she died) that she called his name Benoni: but

his father called him Benjamin.

Here Rachel spoke words of woes and even called her son the son of sorrow because the labour was hard! But the baby's father was wise and quick to change the name to Benjamin because he knew that that singular incident would lead to an un-ending life of disaster and sorrows.

There are many mothers who do not even remember words they spoke while in pain of delivery, however believe it or not those words will influence and shape the course of events in the life of that child. It is also important to note from the above scripture that the father of a child has a strong authority to reverse or cast out negative spirits from a child.

UNDERSTANDING THE BLOOD VEHICLE

It is also worthy to note that all kinds of things can be passed down through the blood line because the Bible states that the life of a man is in the blood. It is not only the physical features of the parents that are passed down to the child. Character traits as well as weaknesses and strengths, can be passed down to a

child. The blood is the vehicle of spirits and traits! The spiritual state of a parent can be passed down to a child, in other words, if there are curses, sicknesses, failures, evil cycles of polygamy or evil trends of all sorts, it can be transferred to a child!
This is important because it implies that demonic influences and issues that make it necessary for children to pass through deliverance ministration are not only postnatal. A child can be born with overwhelming complex generational baggage and evil blood line issues. A child can be born in a state that makes it necessary for him or her to be prayed over for deliverance from birth.

In fact, unless parents have taken action to do a spiritual sanitisation before the baby's birth and have constantly ministered to the baby from conception in the womb, it is almost always the case that babies are given birth to in a state where they need deliverance. I remember the story of a woman who brought her children for deliverance and the problem was that all her three sons were born deaf.
I also remember ministering to a lady who was the sixth in line of children born to her parents. They

were all girls and none of them was married or could marry. This is a clear example of generational spirits that have taken hold of the children in the family.

Once one is alerted to the dangers of passing on weaknesses, infirmities and other unpleasant things to siblings, he should begin breaking curses, destroying legal holds and grounds, and binding any inherited spirits. This is preparation for casting them out. The occult demons are tremendously powerful and tenacious, often staying in families for centuries. People afflicted with them are highly susceptible to psychic phenomena and influence. We have seen children (from babies to teens) receive significant deliverance in the church and at home.

Ex 20:5

Thou shall not bow down thyself to them, nor serve them: for I the Lord thy God am a jealous God, visiting the iniquity of the fathers upon the children unto the third and fourth generation.

The matter becomes more serious when we

consider the above scripture. Here the Bible states that the iniquity or lifestyle and predicaments not just of the parents but of the grandparents to the fourth generation past, can be passed on to children.

This happens not because God is mean and wants to deliberately deposit the problems of the generations past on you or your children but because it is a spiritual principle that every man carries within him three to four generations.

Isa 49:25
But thus saith the Lord, ... for I will contend with him that contendeth with thee, and I will save thy children. I will save thy children.

A generation is a lifespan, which the Bible says is the average of 70 years. This means four generations amounts to 70x4=280years.

In other words issues have occurred and covenants that have been made for over two centuries before, can still affect children born two centuries after.

So a child can be dealing with not only his daddy and mummy's devils but also those of grannies and great grannies!

NEGLIGENCE AND SELFISHNESS OF PARENTS

Sometime ago a lady came to me who never knew her father, her mother got pregnant by a man who took her through a bitter experience, she decided to punish the man and not allow him to ever see his daughter. On the other hand, while the child grew, she lied to her that her father was dead. The girl grew with trauma and pain and could not get a grip on her life and was always afraid of commitments.

One day she went to the hospital for treatment of a fever. Alas the man who treated her was her long lost father allegedly thought dead. The rest was a series of confessions, revelations and joy mixed with pain. The girl confided in me that she found it hard to trust people because her mother had lied to her for thirty years of her life.

This story exemplifies the selfishness of parents many times because of their egocentric behaviour. They forget the devastating effects their decisions can have

on the children involved. They themselves subject their kids to rejection, distrust and hatred, which are foundational spirits for greater levels of demonic activity and problems in the life of a child.

POLYGAMOUS WITCHCRAFT

The problem of polygamy is also related to the issue of selfishness and negligence of parents. When a man who is married with children does not consider the peace of his home and out of selfish lust takes another wife or concubine whose presence and children begins to rival that of the legitimate wife and children, he has exposed his family to both psychological and diabolical afflictions because, in most cases, there will be attempts to exact equal rights to the man's love, attention and estate.

Strife, manipulation, fetish efforts and witchcraft will be employed by either or both parties to surmount one another, and the innocent children of the women involved always end up being the victims of these battles.

Also when women see a married man who already has a wife and think that he is the most ideal person to engage in a relationship, they are asking for trouble

not just for themselves but for their children born and unborn.

PARENTAL RESPONSIBILITY

Pr 22:6

Train up a child in the way he should go; and when he is old, he will not depart from it.

I must commend school teachers and governments alike for theories, efforts and policies used in training and ensuring the well-being, responsible growth and assimilation of children into the system. But I must also quickly state that the responsibility of training a child rests squarely on the shoulders of the parents.

Parents who think that children should be left to the system to train and rear are not living according to God's word. Teachers can help, governments can support but the main responsibility is on the parents.

A man once said that he does not see why his wife was complaining about him neglecting the children; after all, he fulfilled his responsibility of providing
financially for his children and wife. Well that is good but financial provision is not enough; both parents need to be one hundred percent involved in

the upbringing of the child by showing love and guidance to their children.

1 Jo 4:18
There is no fear in love; but perfect love casteth out fear: because fear hath torment. He that feareth is not made perfect in love.

The Bible states that perfect love casteth out fear, and that fear brings affliction, fear is the basis of all kinds of demonic infestation! The Bible states that love is the cure for fear. Parents need to show children love and close the door of low self-esteem, rejection, loneliness and confusion that plagues a child at the different stages of his life.

Neglecting children as they grow gives room to various insecurities in their lives that will serve as access points for demons into their lives. Parents must be discerning and careful of what their children do,
wear, eat and drink as well as with whom they associate as they grow.

A parent who buys a TV and a video for the room of their 13 year old son and have not bought him a single Christian literature before, such as a Bible or Christian movies, is asking for trouble. The same thing goes for a 15 year old daughter who has unlimited privacy in her room and always locks her door and her parents can never access it.

THE POWER OF CHILD DEDICATION (Who your child is bound to determines who he is free from). Lu 2:22

And when the days of her purification according to the Law of Moses were accomplished, they brought him to Jerusalem, to present him to the Lord;
23 (As it is written in the law of the Lord, Every male that openeth the womb shall be called holy to the Lord)

The Bible states here that even baby Jesus was presented to the Lord, even though He was the Lord.

In the real sense the Lord was being presented to the Lord. One of the reasons why God will show us this example, among others, is because He is trying to show us the importance of presenting children to the Lord.

1 Co 7:14 -Else were your children unclean; but

now are they holy.

To be holy means simply to be set apart or dedicated to something, to be consecrated for the use of God. The Bible states here that even if your children were unclean or accessible to any spirit or power when they are dedicated to God, they become holy. In other words, an exclusion clause is placed on their lives for every other user to stay clear!

A prevention order for demons, sickness and affliction of all sorts to stay clear of children is in place once a child is dedicated to God.

An undedicated child can receive invitation or interest from any one or more spirits, but a child dedicated to God becomes holy, and is strictly for the use of God alone!

I was shocked at the parents who gave birth to a child and named the child at home by themselves and forgot all about it. No man of God was invited to pray or dedicate the child to God. When I asked them why, they just said they do not see the need for the ceremony!

Some think that dedicating a child to God in church is a 'ceremony', others think it is unnecessary while others think it is an excuse to spend money to feed church members. Others strictly believe that it is their responsibility to do as they please with their child.

Well Jesus' parents could have taken Him and dedicated Him at home, being Godly people themselves. They brought Him to the temple. There are some events that are reserved for God's servants to do, because they are God's representatives.
If you refuse to dedicate your baby or do them by yourself, the protection and cover over that child is solely you, but a child dedicated to God has heaven's interest and eyes fixed on him!

2Ki 4:17
And the woman conceived, and bare a son at that season that Elisha had said unto her, according to the time of life.
18 And when the child was grown, it fell on a day, that he went out to his father to the reapers.
19 And he said unto his father, my head, and my head. And he said to the lad, Carry him to his mother.

20 And when he had taken him, and brought him to his mother, he sat on her knees till noon, and then died.

In the above excerpt, Elisha had prayed and miraculously the Shunnemite woman had received a child, the boy grew and mysteriously fell sick at the prime of his youth and died! He fell sick in the presence of his father and died right on the lap of his mother!

Such is the kind of attack that the enemy is releasing against children in these times, and like the parents of this boy, many parents do not know where to draw the line when it comes to children related problems as to whether it is spiritually rooted or just physical, the parents watched this boy die right in their presence but they could not do much about it. Thank God for Elisha the prophet. In the same way today, the enemy releases onslaughts against children and many parents are helpless and novices as to spiritual approaches in tackling the enemy in the lives of their children.

In the last days, the devil is waging a serious war

against children knowing fully well that they are leaders of tomorrow.

God has a plan for children, but the devil is out to make sure that plan does not come to pass; when Moses a deliverer is born, there is a destroyer assigned to kill him. Therefore parents have to be wise and sharp in the spirit, seeking deliverance for their children from evil bondages common against children and youths today.

One of the most effective ways of children deliverance is to pray over them when they are asleep.

God wants to use children to defeat the enemy today. That is why the Bible states that out of the mouth of babes and suckling children thou has ordained strength, because of thine enemy that thou might still the enemy and the avenger – **Psalm 8:2.**

The devil knows this plan of God. In fact he knows this scripture so he is on the lookout and uses various social factors and information to foster transmission of social and moral values that act as entry points for demons and strongholds into the lives of children!

Children, as well as adults, are influenced by what they see and what they hear, touch and eat. Children can also be possessed from the womb if the mother goes to strange places where spirits can enter the child in the womb.

Ancestral transfer of spirits and sicknesses such as diabetes, asthma, sickle cell, curses of hardship are also some of the vices to which children have become victims.

Fear, insecurity, physical and sexual abuse could also impact the lives of a child negatively.

The confidence of every parent should be in the scripture that states that: ye are of God little children and have overcome them: because greater is he that is in you than he that is in the world!

NO LONGER SHALL FATHERS EAT GRAPES

Jer. 31:29

In those days they shall say no more, the fathers have eaten a sour grape, and the children's teeth are set on edge.

> Isa 49:25 But thus saith the Lord,… for I will contend with him that contendeth with thee, and I will save thy children. I will save thy children.

1Jo. 4:4
Ye are of God, little children, and have overcome them: because greater is he that is in you, than he that is in the world.

Although the Bible earlier records that God will require the sins of the father from the children to the third and fourth generation, this is because every male seed carries within him three or four generation, so generational curses are transferred, and generational blessings can also be transferred to latter generations. The Bible states that Levi paid tithe in the belly of Abraham.

However when it comes to generational curses, the Bible later states that God will no longer request the sins of the father from the children. In other words, the transfer of evil deposits into the lives of your children can be stopped! The Bible states that no longer shall the fathers eat grapes and the teeth of the children be set upon the edge. I am very excited about this scripture because I believe this is the core scripture and rule that gives us the audacity to stop generational evil transfers in the track! I want you to prophesy this scripture over your children born and unborn, just say ... no longer shall the fathers eat grapes and the teeth of the children be set upon the edge! Say it over them again and again!

DISOBEDIENCE IN CHILDREN
Isa 8:18
Behold, I and the children whom the LORD hath given me are for signs and for wonders in Israel from the LORD of hosts, which dwelleth in mount Zion.

The Bible states that disobedience is as the sin of witchcraft; this means disobedience is a door way for evil spirit to come into children. In fact it is the first sign of demonic activity in a child. In Colossians 3 and Ephesians 5:6 the Bible also uses the term child of disobedience, this implies that disobedience is a by-product and is mostly a carryover of the disobedience to God in the lives of the parents, the first and most effective way to start correcting and overcoming recalcitrance in a child is for the parents to first of all mend their ways with God. That is why the Bible states; children obey your parents in the Lord in Ephesians 6:1. This is not just a commandment, it is a principle, a parent not living according to God's word or who is disobeying God has exposed the children to be possessed by the spirit of disobedience which will form a foundation for other compounding problems and spirit in the life of the child.

The Bible also talks of the spirit that works in the children of disobedience- in other words there is a spirit of disobedience that works! Parents need to cast out this spirit, and this becomes easy when they are also in the Lord, the spirit of disobedience or defiance has no choice but to leave! Parents have the responsibility to bring up their children in the way of the Lord by instruction as well as example. Children learn by observation and emulation so we as parents must live holy and be pacesetters and role models of what we expect of our children.

CHILDREN OF BELIAL
Judges 19:22
Now as they were making their hearts merry, behold, the men of the city, certain sons of Belial...
2 Ki 2:23
And he went up from thence unto Bethel:

and as he was going up by the way, there came forth little children out of the city, and mocked him, and said unto him, Go up, thou bald head; go up, thou bald head.

24 And he turned back, and looked on them, and cursed them in the name of the LORD. And there came forth two she bears out of the wood, and tare forty and two children of them.

In this story, the Bible also states that the children of Belial, were taunting and mocking Prophet Elijah and he cursed them. I believe this is a typology of what our approach should be against the spirit of Belial; a prophetic and aggressive warfare approach!

The spirit of Belial is the spirit of irresponsible and nuisance behaviour in children; it is the spirit of mischief. When a child begins to demonstrate high degree of nuisance behaviour, like sneaking out at night, excessive secrecy, locking doors of the room every minute, bad reports from teachers, truancy from school, funny habits, keeping bad gangs; all of these are examples of the operation of the spirit of

Belial. When you see this operation, you should begin to decree the judgement of God on that spirit and curse it to die out of your children in the name of Jesus.

THE CURSE OF LEVI

De 33:8

And of Levi he said, Let thy Thummim and thy Urim be with the holy one, whim thou didst prove at Massah, and with whom thou didst strive at the waters of Meribah;

9 Who said unto his father and to his mother, I have not seen him; neither did he acknowledge his brethren, <u>nor knew his own children</u>; for they have observed thy word, and kept thy covenant.

Levi represents the servants of God; men and women who have given their lives to serve God. This blessing of Moses over the Levites (servants of God) appears more to have operated like a curse in the lives of many men and women of God! Moses prayed that the Levites will be dedicated to their call so much that they will have no regard or time for their children and family. Like the ostriches neglect his young, this prayer has been more of a curse and a negative trend to men and women of God alike in the Bible. The children of the high priest Eli were rebellious and were like sons of Belial and were the reason for his demise. The same was the case for Samuel's children as well as most of David's children, who were extremely evil, disobedient and rebellious against God's ways and laws.

However I am excited because as we got into the New Testament, I realised that this curse can be broken, and should be broken and taken seriously as a prayer topic by every minister of God over their family.

As a result of this curse, I believe many ministers of God unconsciously neglect their family and children and do not give the necessary attention to welfare and wellbeing of their family. That is why there are so many examples in these modern days of divorce and break down in marriages amongst ministers, wayward and rebellious minister's children etc.

However we have a good example in Timothy whose mother and grandmother were ministers of God. He was probably brought up in a single parent household but grew up in the way of the Lord.

Dear man or woman of God if you are reading this now, you need to break the curse of Levi over your family and begin to pray the blessing of Timothy over your children.

You can break the curse! Your children do not have to be rebellious because you are a minister of God, break the yoke right now! Invoke the blessing of Timothy upon your family now!

PRAYER CONFESSION FOR PARENTS FOR THEIR CHILDREN

... My children are taught of the LORD and great shall be their peace (Isaiah 54:13)

Shield your children properly with the blood of Jesus Christ and ask for God's protection from all attacks of the enemy before proceeding to make this prayer confession.

PRAYER CONFESSION:

In the name of Jesus Christ, I am a covenant child of God; Jesus Christ is my Lord and Saviour. I am born again, sanctified and redeemed in Jesus' name. I am the righteousness of God in Jesus' name, Amen. Because I am in Christ, I am Abraham's seed and heirs according to the promise in Jesus' name. Abraham's blessings are mine. I receive the full benefits of salvation, which Jesus wrought for me on the cross of Calvary, 2000 years ago.

I am a fruitful vine and a joyful mother/father of children in Jesus' name, Amen. Almighty God has established an everlasting covenant for me and my children to obey Him and that His word will never depart from our mouth forever in Jesus' name. The word of God states that children are the heritage of the Lord; my children have been given to me by Almighty God through the Lord Jesus Christ in Jesus' name, Amen.

In Jesus' name, as I pray this prayer confession for my children, I hand over the battle to the Lord, and I received victory in every area of their lives in Jesus' name, Amen. When I am saved, it is for my house and I in Jesus' name. My children are saved and filled with the spirit of God in Jesus' name, Amen. I hand over my children to the Lord Jesus Christ for protection for no man shall be able to pluck them out of His hand in Jesus' name, Amen. Right now, I bind every workmanship of the devil and his followers against my children in the name of Jesus Christ, Amen. I lose their spirit, soul and body from every captivity, prison gate, yokes, or possession, is they in the spiritual or in the physical in Jesus' name, Amen. I send the power that is in the Word of God to run swiftly into their spirit, soul and body to free them from this oppression in Jesus' name, Amen.

I lose the Angels of God to encamp round about my children and to deliver them from every attack of the enemy in Jesus' name, Amen. The Lord Jesus Christ has given His angels charge over my children and as the wall surround Jerusalem, they encamp roundabout them to deliver them, they fight for them; they watch over them, they protect them from all my enemies in Jesus' name, Amen. My children are established in righteousness and they are far from oppression in Jesus' name, Amen. No weapon formed against them shall prosper in Jesus' name. Right now I command

> Isa 49:25 But thus saith the Lord,... for I will contend with him that contendeth with thee, and I will save thy children. I will save thy children.

every oppression of principalities and powers of the devil against my children to be destroyed. I send the fire of the Holy Ghost to consume every plot of witchcraft and marine attacks against them in Jesus name, Amen. I destroy every agreement or covenant between my children and any spiritual or physical agent of the devil, I cut off every link with the kingdom of darkness in Jesus name. I command a separation order now between my children and all agents of the devil. My children have been dedicated to Jesus Christ and are children of light. When the enemy seeks them, they will not find them for they are hidden in the mighty hand of Jehovah in Jesus' name. Amen.

In the name of Jesus Christ, I destroy every association of witches and wizards, marine spirits and all the powers of the devil against my children. The Word of God is quick and powerful and can discern the thoughts and intents of the heart, in Jesus name, I send the power in the Word of God to expose any plot or device of the devil and his agents to lure my children through deceit into any evil associations and gathering in their sleep or awake. I command the assembly, associations or gatherings

> Isa 49:25 But thus saith the Lord,… for I will contend with him that contendeth with thee, and I will save thy children. I will save thy children.

INHERITANCE
Blessing and Responsibilities
Ps 127:3

Lo, children are an heritage of the LORD: and the fruit of the womb is his reward. 4 As arrows are in the hand of a mighty man; so are children of the youth. 5 Happy is the man that hath his quiver full of them: they shall not be ashamed, but they shall speak with the enemies in the gate.

This above scripture clearly expresses the fact that just as we do not have to pay for an inheritance that comes from our parents, it is the same way children are free gifts from God. However, each inheritance comes with blessings and responsibilities. In the same manner, God expects parents to be spiritually responsible for their children. Some people say that children do not need deliverance. I could not disagree more. Parents have a solemn responsibility to provide
protection for their offspring in the matter of spiritual warfare. So many curses, legal holds,

and other legal

grounds can be inherited through the ignorance, curiosity and/or wilful disobedience of the parent. In addition to the above, our society provides a climate for demon infestation.

An inheritance is surely a pedestal to him who receives it. In other words, you begin to enjoy and live in the labour of another: an inheritance increases your wealth and strength.

In the same way children are an inheritance given by God to us, as a pedestal to lift us up, that is why the Bible states in verse 5 of the passage above that children are like arrows in the hand of a mighty man. In other words, our child is meant to project us and cross boundaries that we cannot cross and reach heights that we could not reach in our youthful days. Unfortunately for many parents, children have

become a burden and a snare, almost like a curse to them, some because their children have grown up bringing them into disrepute, others because the enemy has attacked their children with ill health and thus made them a constant burden with no peace of mind to the parents.

Others have not met the expectations of their parents and that of God for their lives; instead their many strides of success have been coloured dark with failure and multiple errors at different stages. Some children are unable to complete what they start; some drop out of school and some join bad gangs or are even initiated into cults or secret societies.

The reason for these and many more woes that befall children is not farfetched because the answer is in that passage above. Firstly, the Bible calls children an inheritance from God; like most inheritances, there will be factors that will contend and contest the right of the parents to receive this blessing.

Secondly, the Bible states they are like arrows. An arrow is an offensive weapon. The enemy knows that and will not watch you build up dangerous arsenals to devastate him eventually. This fact is very interesting because it clearly implies that the fact that children are born is proof that the adversary has vested interest in them, to make sure that they do not become effective enough to be a threat to his kingdom.

He therefore attacks children with all sorts to afflict them and cripple their destiny!
The same scripture expatiates further by saying that our children are born to speak with the enemies at the gate!

In the Bible days, the cities had gates and wise men and magistrates sat at the gates of the cities to settle disputes. Creditors also waited at the gate, to lend money and ask for money owed to them. In the former situation children were witnesses in judicial courts, also children were proof of credit worthiness.

There were also pirates outside the gates of the city seeking to attack merchants travelling in and out of the city; a man with children had strength and power to resist the enemy. The enemy knows this and will fight tooth and nail to make sure that your children cannot stand against him.

PHAROAH ON THE RAMPAGE
Catch them young (while they are upon the stool) Ex 1:16

And he said, When ye do the office of a midwife to the Hebrew women, and see them upon the stools; if it be a son, then ye shall kill him: but if it be a daughter, then she shall live.

The Bible tells us here that pharaoh commanded children to be killed at the point of delivery; here we see the enemy launching an attack against children from the infant stage (WHILE ON THE STOOL), this spirit of pharaoh is still on the rampage today.

I was driving one day and I saw little kids being led by their teacher from school on a trip somewhere. When

I asked where they were going, the teacher told me they were going to see the latest witchcraft sensation movie.

This irony is amazing because, in these same schools, prayers and expressions of love for Jesus have been banned. Our children are being taught and schooled in witchcraft but are told that mentioning the name of Jesus is offensive.

This is why we have problems with parents who do not see anything wrong with their children celebrating Halloween (a witchcraft festival) but have problems with bringing their children to church.

For some, their children have all kinds of toys and books about evil and witchcraft but not a single Bible story book.

The enemy is on a rampage to catch our children young; the battle is on whether or not you believe it. You must take hold of the weapons of war and fight the inevitable battle for both the sanctity of your home and deliverance of your children! If parents wait until the child is grown up before attempting deliverance, they will discover the enemy has wasted no time and has burrowed in deeply, often scarring body and mind. They will work tirelessly to put a child in bondage, drag him out into the world, and enslave him with many sinful habits. An ounce of prevention here is certainly worth the proverbial 'pound of cure'.

There are many ways the enemy tries to catch children young, and demonize, possess or pervert their destiny-some of which we will examine.

NEED FOR CHILDREN'S DELIVERANCE
Gen 3:16

Unto the woman he said, I will greatly multiply thy sorrow and thy conception; in sorrow thou shalt bring forth children; and thy desire shall be to thy husband, and he shall rule over thee.

The Bible states here that there is pain in conception as well as in childbirth, because of the pains and discomfort that surround conception, many women utter words of woes while they are pregnant and all these words have a great level of influence upon the destiny of children.

This is the reason why pregnant women must learn to speak to the baby in their womb, read the bible to them, and speak prophetic words to them in the womb.

> Isa 49:25 But thus saith the Lord,... for I will contend with him that contendeth with thee, and I will save thy children. I will save thy children.

1) Lord, I thank you for the work of creation you have started in me.

2) Lord perfect your good work of creation that you have started in me.

3) I command every part of my body to function perfectly for the formation of this baby in Jesus' name.

4) I claim divine health during and after the pregnancy in Jesus' name.

5) Blood of Jesus, be transfused into my blood.

6) I claim the life in the blood of Jesus for my baby and I in Jesus' name.

7) Lord envelope me and my baby with your fire in Jesus' name.

> Isa 49:25 But thus saith the Lord,... for I will contend with him that contendeth with thee, and I will save thy children. I will save thy children.

8) I receive the strength of God to carry and deliver safely in Jesus' name.

TUESDAY

9) I stand against any malfunction and abnormality in my baby in Jesus' name.

10) I stand against any form of abortion or premature delivery in Jesus' name.

11) I break all the curses placed upon my children's head in Jesus' name.

12) I break every covenant my parents have made with the earth or spirit husband in the name of Jesus.

13) I break all family curses in Jesus' name.

14) I break every covenant I made with the earth and spirit husband in Jesus' name.

> Isa 49:25 But thus saith the Lord,... for I will contend with him that contendeth with thee, and I will save thy children. I will save thy children.

15) Lord envelope me and my baby with your fire in Jesus' name.

WEDNESDAY

16) I break every evil covenant in my life consciously or unconsciously.

17) I break every conscious/unconscious covenant with the spirit of death in Jesus' name.

18) I break all curses placed on me by my elders/head.

19) I break every covenant that my parents have made on my behalf with any demonic powers in Jesus' name.

20) I break every covenant that I have made with the earth and spirit husband in Jesus' name.

21) I break all family curses in Jesus' name.

22) Lord envelope me and my baby with your fire in the name of Jesus.

THURSDAY

23) Lord let the blood of Jesus flush out any poison I might have taken consciously or unconsciously in the name of Jesus.

24) I drink the blood of Jesus and eat the fire of the Holy Ghost.

25) I soak myself and my baby in the blood of Jesus.

26) You my baby, receive the fire of God in Jesus' name.

27) You eaters of flesh and drinkers of blood, begin to eat your own flesh and drink your own blood in Jesus' name.

28) All dead and dying cells of my body and my baby should receive the power of resurrection in Jesus' name.

29) Lord envelope me and my baby with your fire in Jesus' name.

FRIDAY

30) You stubborn pursuers of my life, begin to die after the order of Pharaoh.

31) You enemies of progress in my life, receive destruction after the order of Herod.

32) All those who are gathered against me, receive confusion and be scattered by the thunder fire of God.

33) You stubborn pursuers of my life, begin to die after the order of Pharaoh.

34) You enemies of progress in my life, receive destruction after the order of Herod.

35) All those who are gathered against me, receive confusion and be scattered by the thunder fire of God after the order of the tower of Babel.

36) Any evil trap planted in my womb contrary to to perfect development and growth of my baby be uprooted and roasted in Jesus' name.

37) No weapon formed against me or my baby shall prosper in Jesus' name.

38) I refuse every divination, spell or enchantment issued against me.

39) Lord envelope me and my baby with your fire in Jesus' name.

> Isa 49:25 But thus saith the Lord,… for I will contend with him that contendeth with thee, and I will save thy children. I will save thy children.

SATURDAY

40) Lord, turn me and my baby into untouchable coals of fire in Jesus' name.

41) Make me and my baby wind of fire against the enemy.

42) I consume with fire all evil altars with evil sacrifices made by demonic priests and counsellors against me.

43) Lord, keep busy all agents of the devil at home and hospital waiting for the day of my delivery to drink my blood in Jesus' name.

44) I bind you strongman over my life.

45) I loose myself from the stronghold of the strongman over my life in Jesus' name.

46) Lord envelope me and my baby with your

fire and Jesus' name.

SUNDAY

47) Lord turn my breast milk into the blood of Jesus.

48) My baby will not reject my breast milk in the name of Jesus.

49) I reject all complication during child bearing and after child bearing in Jesus' name.

50) I command my cervix to be fully dilated and the passage big and open enough for safe delivery of my baby in Jesus' name.

51) I command all evil monitors of my pregnancy and its progress to receive blindness and spiritual paralysis in Jesus' name.

Isa 49:25 But thus saith the Lord,... for I will contend with him that contendeth with thee, and I will save thy children. I will save thy children.

52) My baby and I shall be alive and well to bless the name of the Lord in Jesus' name.

53) Lord envelope me and my baby with your fire.

Isa 49:25 But thus saith the Lord,... for I will contend with him that contendeth with thee, and I will save thy children. I will save thy children.

120
PRAYERS THAT WILL SECURE THE DESTINIES OF YOUR CHILDREN AND AVERT PROBLEMS AT VARIOUS STAGES IN THE LIVES OF CHILDREN

De 28:7
The LORD shall cause thine enemies that rise up against thee to be smitten before thy face: they shall come out against thee one way and they shall flee before thee seven ways.

Isa 8:18
Behold I and the children whom the LORD hath given me are for signs and wonders in Israel from the LORD of hosts, which dwelleth in mount Zion.

1) Any power that wants me to cry over my children, you are a liar; die in the name of Jesus.

2) Every curse passed down from children to parents working against the life of my children be cancelled in the name of Jesus.

> Isa 49:25 But thus saith the Lord,... for I will contend with him that contendeth with thee, and I will save thy children. I will save thy children.

3) Every evil covenant in my bloodline influencing the life of my children -be broken in the name of Jesus.

4) I break the power of every spirit militating against (mention your child's name) in the name of Jesus.

5) Let the blood of Jesus cleanse the mind, soul, emotions, body and spirit of (mention your child's name) in the name of Jesus.

6) All inherited problems passed down to my children from my family line, be destroyed in Jesus' name.

7) Every spirit of pride and stubbornness that the enemy has released against my children, I command you to be destroyed in the name of Jesus.

> Isa 49:25 But thus saith the Lord,... for I will contend with him that contendeth with thee, and I will save thy children. I will save thy children.

8) Whatever plans the enemy has made to make it impossible for my children to serve the Lord, I frustrate those plans in the name of Jesus.

9) Every bloodline curse that might have been passed down to my children by my lineage or my spouse's lineage be destroyed in the name of Jesus.

10) Every bloodline covenant that might have been passed down to my children by my lineage or my

11) spouse's lineage be destroyed in the name of Jesus.

12) Every inherited and generational problem passed down to my children from me or my spouse's lineage be destroyed in the name of Jesus.

> Isa 49:25 But thus saith the Lord,... for I will contend with him that contendeth with thee, and I will save thy children. I will save thy children.

13) O God arise and let my children become........) say what you want your children to become and say their name one after the other).

14) You demonic arrow of abnormal fears fired against my children: come out and return to your sender in the name of Jesus.

15) You demonic arrow of familiar spirits fired against my children: come out and return to your sender in the name of Jesus.

16) You demonic arrow of sexual lust fired against my children, come out and return to your sender in the name of Jesus.

17) You demonic arrow of addiction, fired against my children; come out and return to your sender in the name of Jesus.

18) You demonic arrow of unreasonable silence

> Isa 49:25 But thus saith the Lord,... for I will contend with him that contendeth with thee, and I will save thy children. I will save thy children.

fired against my children, come out and return to your sender in the name of Jesus.

19) You demonic arrow of anger fired against my children, come out and return to your sender in the name of Jesus.

20) You demonic arrow of forgetfulness fired against my children, come out and return to your sender in the name of Jesus.

21) You demonic arrow of rebellion fired against my children, come out and return to your sender in the name of Jesus.

22) You demonic arrow of mind darkness fired against my children, come out and return to your sender in the name of Jesus.

23) You demonic arrow of confusion fired against my children, come out and return to your sender in the name of Jesus.

> Isa 49:25 But thus saith the Lord,... for I will contend with him that contendeth with thee, and I will save thy children. I will save thy children.

24) You demonic arrow of day dreaming fired against my children, come out and return to your sender in the name of Jesus.

25) My children will not become the society's black sheep or a negative example in the name of Jesus.

26) Any bad or negative influence and control over my children be broken in the name of Jesus.

27) Negative influence and problems in my children, created as a result of being born in an undesired gender of the parents, be destroyed by the power in the blood of Jesus.

28) Negative influence and problem in my children created as a result of certain deformities, be destroyed by the power in the blood of Jesus.

29) Negative influence and problems in my children created as a result of sexual aggression by their father to their mother in the presence of the child, be destroyed by the power in the blood of Jesus.

30) Negative influence and problem in my children created as a result of being sent to boarding school; be destroyed by the power in the blood of Jesus.

31) Negative influence and problems in my children created as a result of attempted abortion during pregnancy, be destroyed by the power in the blood of Jesus.

32) Any ungodly, unprofitable and adverse relationship or friendship that the enemy has prepared for my children, be frustrated in the name of Jesus.

> Isa 49:25 But thus saith the Lord,… for I will contend with him that contendeth with thee, and I will save thy children. I will save thy children.

33) I disconnect my children from every negative association and grouping in the name of Jesus.

34) I frustrate every evil initiation attempt over the life of my children in the name of Jesus.

35) The strongman assigned to derail my children- I bind and derail you in the name of Jesus.

36) Any strange and evil power interested in my children be paralysed in the name of Jesus.

37) Let every evil connection between my children and ancestral spirits be broken in the name of Jesus.

38) Any power assigned to monitor the progress of my children for evil, receive blindness in the name of Jesus.

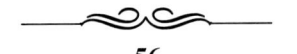

> Isa 49:25 But thus saith the Lord,… for I will contend with him that contendeth with thee, and I will save thy children. I will save thy children.

39) You (mention your child's name) I disconnect you from every evil conscious grouping in the name of Jesus.

40) You (mention your child's name) I disconnect you from every evil association and friendship in the name of Jesus.

41) You (mention your child's name) I disconnect you from every evil unconscious grouping in the name of Jesus.

42) You (mention your child's name) be released from the prison of the strong man of failure and death in the name of Jesus.

43) Lord, destroy everything in my children that is stopping them from doing your will in the name of Jesus.

44) Lord perfect your good work of creation in me in the name of Jesus.

> Isa 49:25 But thus saith the Lord,… for I will contend with him that contendeth with thee, and I will save thy children. I will save thy children.

45) Every covenant of death associated with the age of (mention your child's name) be broken in the name of Jesus.

46) Every covenant of death associated with the place of birth of (mention your child's name) be broken in the name of Jesus.

47) Enemies trying to get my children because they cannot get me receive disgrace in the name of Jesus.

48) Enemies of my home, scatter by fire in the name of Jesus.

49) Any strange woman speaking failure over my children, be silenced by the blood of Jesus.

50) Thou influence of strange women over my children, be broken in the name of Jesus.

> Isa 49:25 But thus saith the Lord,… for I will contend with him that contendeth with thee, and I will save thy children. I will save thy children.

51) Any power that wants to convert my child to a public nuisance be completely paralysed in Jesus' name.

52) You demonic arrow of slowness fired against my children, come out and return to your sender in the name of Jesus.

53) You demonic arrow of stupidity fired against my children, come out and return to your sender in the name of Jesus.

54) You demonic arrow of inactivity fired against my children, come out and return to your sender in the name of Jesus.

55) You demonic arrow of inability to read, fired against my children, come out and return to your sender in the name of Jesus.

56) You demonic arrow of infirmity fired against

my children, come out and return to your sender in the name of Jesus.

57) You demonic arrow of indifference fired against my children, come out and return to your sender in the name of Jesus.

58) You demonic arrow of dullness fired against my children, come out and return to your sender in the name of Jesus.

59) You demonic arrow of bad sleeping and nightmares fired against my children, come out and return to your sender in the name of Jesus.

60) Negative influence and problem in my children created as a result of insufficient affection and love in the family, be destroyed by the power in the blood of Jesus.

61) Negative influence and problem in my

children created as a result of unjust punishment and discipline, be destroyed by the power in the blood of Jesus.

62) Negative influence and problem in my children created as a result of sexual molestation be destroyed by the power in the blood of Jesus.

63) Negative influence and problems in my children created as a result of inferiority complex and negative comments from parents and relatives, be destroyed by the power in the blood of Jesus.

64) Any power that wants to convert my child to a failure be completely paralysed in Jesus' name.

65) Negative influence and problem created in my children as a result of over pampering; be destroyed by the power in the blood of Jesus.

> Isa 49:25 But thus saith the Lord,... for I will contend with him that contendeth with thee, and I will save thy children. I will save thy children.

66) Negative influence and problem created in my children as a result of encountering traumatic events and natural disasters; be destroyed by the power in the blood of Jesus.

67) Negative influence and problem created in my children as a result of sudden drop in family standard of living; be destroyed by the power in the blood of Jesus.

68) Negative influence and problem created in my children as a result of lack of faith in a child's sincerity and integrity; be destroyed by the power in the blood of Jesus.

69) Negative influence and problem created in my children as a result of constant criticism by parent; be destroyed by the power in the blood of Jesus.

70) Any power speaking confusion into the lives

of my children; be silenced in the name of Jesus.

71) Every arrow of sudden death of career fired against my children, go back to sender in the name of Jesus.

72) Every spirit of failure fired into the life of my children; be rendered powerless in the name of Jesus.

73) I thank you O Lord for blessing me with (mention your child's name) in the name of Jesus.

74) Lord, I thank you because you will make (metion your child's name) an envy of many generations and an example of good things in Jesus' name.

75) I forbid any sickness or plague from coming upon (mention your child's name) in the

> Isa 49:25 But thus saith the Lord,... for I will contend with him that contendeth with thee, and I will save thy children. I will save thy children.

name of Jesus.

76) I prophesy health and soundness of mind and spirit upon (mention your child's name) in the name of Jesus.

77) (Mention your child's name), hear the word of the Lord; You must not inherit any evil thing from my own family and my blood or from my spouse's family and blood in the name of Jesus.

78) (mention your child's name) I cover you with the blood of Jesus.

79) All the organs and parts of (mention your child's name) body, soul and spirit shall be whole sound and perfect in the name of Jesus.

80) Let the angels of God and the fire of God surround all my children in the name of

> Isa 49:25 But thus saith the Lord,... for I will contend with him that contendeth with thee, and I will save thy children. I will save thy children.

Jesus.

81) You my child, (mention your child's name) refuse to receive or agree with the spirit of failure or infirmity in the name of Jesus.

82) Bladder, respiratory, digestive, circulatory systems of (mention your child's name); I soak you in the blood of Jesus. You will not malfunction or breakdown now or in the future in the name of Jesus.

83) You my child (mention your child's name) receive deliverance and accept the Lord as your saviour at an early age in the name of Jesus.

84) My child (mention your child's name) I pray for you to receive the Holy spirit and be baptised in power in the name of Jesus.

85) Every negative hereditary trait in my

> Isa 49:25 But thus saith the Lord,… for I will contend with him that contendeth with thee, and I will save thy children. I will save thy children.

children- be wiped out by the blood of Jesus.

86) Any series of events, actions and occurrences in the past, present and future that will prevent my children from being a blessing to me and to this world at large, be destroyed in the name of Jesus.

87) Every yoke upon my children as a result of long and protracted labour or cursing words from

88) the mother during delivery, be broken in the name of Jesus.

89) Every yoke upon my children as a result of birth by caesarean section is broken in the name of Jesus

90) Every yoke upon my children as a result of being born with the cord around the neck, be broken in the name of Jesus.

91) Every yoke upon my children as a result of parental separation, divorce or sudden death of one of the parents or grandparents, be broken by the blood of Jesus.

92) Every yoke upon my children born and yet unborn as a result of polygamous witchcraft, be broken by the blood of Jesus.

93) Every yoke upon my children, as a result of parental addiction and sinful habits, be broken by the blood of Jesus.

94) Every yoke upon my children, born or unborn as a result of pregnancy or outside wedlock, be broken by the blood of Jesus.

95) Every yoke upon my children born as a result of accidental pregnancy or rape, be broken by the blood of Jesus.

96) Every yoke upon my children as a result of

rejection and unwanted pregnancy be broken by the blood of Jesus.

97) Every spirit of affliction fired into the life of my children: be rendered powerless in the name of Jesus.

98) Every spirit of failure sent into the life of my children, be rendered powerless in the name of Jesus.

99) Every spirit of bad luck send into the life of my children, be rendered powerless in the name of Jesus.

100) Every spirit of disappointment at the edge of breakthrough, sent into the life of my children; be rendered powerless in the name of Jesus.

101) You witchcraft interest fashioned against my children, be frustrated in the name of

Jesus.

102) Any arrow fired against my children, be frustrated in the name of Jesus.

103) My sons, my daughters, refuse the summoning of witchcraft in the name of Jesus.

104) Every satanic calling, ordained for my children to make them into what the devil wants them to be is scattered in the name of Jesus.

105) Every battle of a male child facing my son, scatter in the name of Jesus.

106) Any power planning to punish me with child loss, my God shall frustrate your plan; you shall be disgraced in the name of Jesus.

107) Any power calling the name of my children

for evil, be silenced in the name of Jesus.

108) (Mention the name of your children); you will not respond to evil summons from the dream in the name of Jesus.

109) (Mention the name of your children); you will not respond to evil peer pressure in the name of Jesus.

110) (Mention the name of your children); you will not respond to any evil physical summons from the dream in the name of Jesus.

111) Any power waiting to dance to the tune of of my cry over my children you shall wait in vain in the name of Jesus.

112) Negative dreams about my children be wiped off by the blood of Jesus.

> Isa 49:25 But thus saith the Lord,... for I will contend with him that contendeth with thee, and I will save thy children. I will save thy children.

113) Negative influence and problem in my children created as a result of harsh parenting be destroyed by the power in the blood of Jesus.

114) You demonic arrow of rejection, fired against my children, come out and return to your sender in the name of Jesus

115) Any bad spirit that may be in the life of (mention your child's name) become powerless in the name of Jesus.

116) You demonic arrow of sleep walking and sleep-talking , fired against my children; come out and return to your sender in the name of Jesus.

117) You power setting a date for the termination of my children, you will fail by fire in the name of Jesus.

118) Any satanic time table for the life of my

children, be broken in the name of Jesus.

119) Original purpose of God for the life of (mention the name of your children) manifest in the name of Jesus.

120) Resources of heaven arise; support the destiny of my children in the name of Jesus.

121) My father in heaven fill all my children with joy, let them reach the fulfilment of their destiny; make them your joy and the joy of their parents and the joy of the world in the name of Jesus.

122) I thank you O Lord for answers to my prayers.